BE THAT CONF

A GUIDE TO SUCCESSFUL ADOLESCENCE

BIBIANA MBUH TAKU

Bibiana Mbuh Taku

ISBN: 9781687010728

Imprint: Independently published

DEDICATION

To Laura & Gavriella

You are the confident girls that I dream about.

You are the motivation behind this book.

Bibiana Mbuh Taku

To My mother, Helen ATABONG ASABA

Thank you for being the epitome of a confident woman. You role-modeled self-confidence to me and that's why I am the resilient confident woman that I am.

Be that confident girl

Go forth and bloom

TABLE OF CONTENTS

BE THAT CONFIDENT GIRL...i

DEDICATION..iii

TABLE OF CONTENTS..vi

FOREWORD 1

PREFACE 8

LET'S TALK CONFIDENCE...13

THE GIRL'S CONFIDENCE CURVE 21

CONFIDENCE LEVEL: SELF-ASSESSMENT 28

CLOSING YOUR GAP 39

PARENTS: COACH, MENTOR, ROLE MODEL 49

ARE YOU A CONFIDENT GIRL? 69

ACKNOWLEDGMENTS..78

ABOUT THE AUTHOR..80

FOREWORD

BE THAT CONFIDENT GIRL is a handbook, which contains resources and tools that if used diligently can effectively support the confidence building of tween and teenage girls.

As an educationist who has spent many years molding young people, I have first-hand experience in the challenges of helping students going through adolescent crisis. Quite often, with the best of intentions, the school administration may not be well equipped or adequately prepared to assess, coach, mentor or successfully counsel some of the children going through a period of low self-confidence crisis. Some of the crisis may be aggravated by peer pressure and bullying that is ever present in every school environment. If the situation is Inadequately or poorly managed it could lead to some of the young people dropping out of school or indulging in criminal activities such as alcohol, drug abuse and violence.

The case of the female gender requires special attention as changes that take place in their physiological development at the beginning and during adolescence have higher negative impact on their self-confidence. For each category of teenage youths there is need for appropriate resources and programs that schools can use to assist the young people to transform these challenges into opportunities to boost their declining self-confidence and emerge as successful strong creative and innovative leaders.

As a father who has raised biological daughters and many family and natural daughters, I can testify to the fact that appropriate and adequate parenting is indispensable in building the self-confidence of young people. Role-modeling, coaching, mentoring and counseling is required to support children through challenges in the various developmental phases.

However, parents are quite often ill-prepared or unaware of the inevitable presence of the challenges. In fact, many parents are usually embarrassed by the indicators of low self-confidence and the resulting crisis such as vulnerability to peer pressure, alcohol abuse, dishonesty, sexual promiscuity, drug abuse, delinquency, early pregnancy, bullying and conflictual relationship with their kids. Parents need to be educated and sensitized through programs and appropriate resources on how to be prepared and proactively use good parenting techniques to coach, mentor, role-model and counsel their children during the vulnerable phase to boost their self-confidence.

Many resources and programs exist that can be used to assist vulnerable teenage children to boost their self-confidence by successfully addressing adolescent challenges. However, there is need to customize some of the resources to the needs of various categories of young persons and the gender perspective is spot-on.

BE THAT CONFIDENT GIRL is proposing a pragmatic approach to assessing and addressing the teenage girl's self-confidence gaps such as:

- Self-assessment;

- Closing the identified confidence gaps through self-coaching;

- Anticipating and closing the confidence gaps through appropriate parenting techniques such as role-modeling, coaching, mentoring and counseling;

- Seeking expert/experience counseling services to close self-confidence gaps and repair any damage caused;

- Peer mentoring.

The proposed tools for self-assessment are user-friendly as well as the suggested tips.

I highly recommend this as a must-read handbook to all teenage girls and in fact all girls, parents and schools. It is very useful to boys who are expected to be supportive to their peers of opposite gender and society at large.

Samuel T. Welang

Bibiana Mbuh Taku

Educationist, Author of "The Essentials of Economics" and an Entrepreneur

PREFACE

An essential and indispensable life skill that defines the personality of a girl in her ability to become a successful leader is self-confidence. I grew up in an era when a girl-child who displayed signs of self-confidence was viewed as naughty, arrogant and less suitable for a wife. This perception was detrimental to the emergence of female leaders as the girl-child was raised mainly for the purpose of marriage.

The confident girl was hence perceived as a potential failure. Such perceptions played a vital role in the parenting of the girl-child whose self-confidence and creative instincts were consciously suppressed. This reduced her opportunities and zeal to develop leadership skills, and therefore the chance to become tomorrow's successful leader.

This gap in the number of potential successful female leaders vs. actual successful female leaders is still ongoing and not limited to the context in which I grew up. Studies have demonstrated that globally more women fall short of achieving their fullest potential in leadership than their male peers.

A frequently suggested deficiency is their self-confidence. While this issue may have evolved, it is just as tangible in the fifties and sixties, as it is today at the village, national and global levels.

I am convinced by my experience as a mother who has raised many daughters and as a grandmother to two precious granddaughters, that self-confidence can be cultivated and instilled into the girl-child as early as her infancy; through appropriate parenting and an enabling psycho-social environment.

Formal education, coaching and mentoring are some of the approaches and methods that can be used to equip the girl-child with this skill which is indispensable for the development of the confident, creative and innovative female leader that our world dearly needs.

"BE THAT CONFIDENT GIRL" is my contribution towards the development of more successful female leaders by placing pertinent content and tips at the disposal of all stakeholders.

This book is my contribution towards the building of a breed of very self-confident female leaders through coaching, role-modeling and mentoring.

Bibiana MBUH TAKU

Self-esteem & Self-efficacy

LET'S TALK CONFIDENCE

Stand for yourself when no one else will. Dream &
achieve on your own terms.

Self-confidence is generally understood as a feeling and demonstration of self-assurance, self-trust and faith in one's abilities. It is a conscious or unconscious demonstration of high self-esteem, self-worth and competence to take charge of situations, even difficult situations, without resulting to self-pity or self-seeking.

Self-confidence is one of the most important components of resilience and it's a skill that every leader must possess. It is a life skill because it gives you the ability and "positive energy" required to effectively deal with challenges that are part and parcel of life.

Self-confidence can be broken into its two main components:

- Self-esteem: The regard or respect that you have for yourself.
- Self-efficacy: Feelings, beliefs and perceptions regarding your abilities to deal with challenges.

12

Every human being needs self-confidence as a skill not only to lead others but most importantly to lead themselves. The girl-child needs the skill even more because the challenges that come with being the female gender are enormous and these challenges start right from birth due to some cultural and societal biases and values. Some of these challenges impair the ability of the girl-child to acquire the skills in any other way except through support in the form of coaching, role modeling or mentoring. Some of these biases and challenges could deal near fatal blow to the self-esteem and self-efficacy of the girl-child requiring special counselling programs for rehabilitation and the development of the girl's self-confidence.

There is a great need for appropriate coaching and mentoring programs to be designed and used to support the self-confidence capacity building of girls. Some of them can be embedded into school curriculums while some could be special programs available as social services in schools, communities or offered by specialized coaches and mentors. Some peer mentoring programs could be managed by schools or offered as "After school" skills development and optional social services for teenage girls.

In subsequent chapters, we shall attempt to provide tips to the young girl and teenage, to assist her to diagnose her self-confidence gaps, as well as self-coaching tips to close the gaps. We shall suggest some parenting tips or guides to parents to use in building the self-confidence of their daughters especially through the vulnerable age with appropriate, coaching, mentoring and role-modelling customized to each context. Finally, it is always necessary to seek expert coaching and mentoring services from experienced and trusted consultants. Of course, a

Be that confident girl

successful teenage could empower others through

peer counseling.

Be proactive: Start when they are young

THE GIRL'S CONFIDENCE CURVE

Let the impact of your fall stimulate the achiever in you: arise & thrive.

It has been observed that Confidence levels vary with age and the confidence levels of male are generally higher than those of their female peers.

While the confidence level of both genders drops sharply from the beginning of puberty, the male gender picks up and has a steady rise while that of the female picks up and fluctuates between stagnation and growth.

The chart below resulting from a survey carried out by "Pulse for Millennial research" in the U.S.A shows that the girl's confidence is lowest at 14 years when it falls below 30% and rises in a zig-zag manner and hits a maximum of 40% at about 32 years. That of her male counterpart rises steadily after the age 14 years and reaches 55% at the age of 32 years:

Be that confident girl

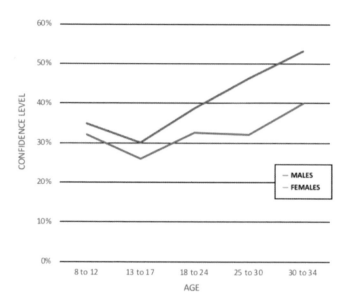

Between the ages of 13 and14 girls experience their lowest confidence level and are very susceptible to peer-pressure. The confidence in their ability to make new friends is 27% lower than boys hence a high risk of feeling rejected, vulnerability to bullying and even suicidal urges.

The result of this study implies that there is a need for appropriate programs to be put in place to proactively address confidence boosting needs of girls, aligned to the issues that typically and adversely affect their confidence levels within the various age brackets: 8 to 14 years and 24 to 30 years.

These coaching and mentoring programs will coach and guide them through challenges that could lead to self-doubt, drop in self-worth and self-esteem. The symptoms of these challenges include feeling stressed, anxious, shy, emotional, worried, depressed and ugly and sometimes suicidal. The fear of failure among early teenage girls is high, and if performance expectations are set unreasonably too high the fears could increase.

Parenting tips and strategies of teenage girls need to be customized to proactively address these challenges using coaching, role modelling and mentoring to boost self-confidence. Such programs need to be aligned with the developmental goals of the girls that may include career, entrepreneurship, leadership, personal development and their overall wellbeing.

However, self-coaching is one of the most effective approaches that could be used to close confidence gap. Therefore, it is important for the girl-child to be given opportunities to assess her confidence level and above all acquire self-coaching skills to address gaps.

Trust yourself and be in charge

CONFIDENCE LEVEL: SELF-ASSESSMENT

How high is your self-confidence? Check the height of each indicator

Do you know your self-confidence level? We have gathered indicators of high self-confidence, which can guide you to identify the area, which contributes most to your confidence level gap.

Self-confidence Assessment quiz

Self-Confidence assessment question	Yes	No	Comments
You can easily say what your top three achievements or strongest skills are.			
You are comfortable talking about yourself			
You don't spend much time analyzing what other people think about you			
You don't try to be perfect			
You are not afraid to step outside your comfort zone to learn new things			
You rarely compare yourself to others (even in your mind)			
You hang out with people who encourage you and lift you up			
You are comfortable turning to trusted friends and family for help			
You have leisure or extra-curricular activities			
You don't mind speaking in front of many people			
You sleep well			
You have a hobby that helps you relax			
You don't take other people's problems and opinions personally			
You are not afraid of rejection			
You take criticism as an opportunity to grow			
You make friends easily			

You don't take rejection personally and instead look for the next opportunity			
You consider failure as a lesson learnt and don't allow it to define you			
You have a mentor or role model			
You are able to forgive past hurts			
You easily praise people for their achievements			
You graciously accept compliments			

Each negative answer indicates a gap that needs to be addressed. In the comments column you can indicate the action you want to take to transform the **NO** to a YES or at least to manage it.

The above questions are based on the following high self-esteem and self-efficacy indicators:

- **You have a feeling of wholeness:** you can pull out control and confidence from within and not from any external factors. You can take charge of your emotional, physical, mental and spiritual wellbeing.

- **You show gratitude:** You recognize your strengths and know how to manage your weaknesses so that they do not become liabilities. You focus on things that matter most. You appreciate your blessings and do not dwell on things that you lack. You accept criticisms and compliments graciously, you return compliments, acknowledge everyone's worth and show appreciation to them.

- **You are competitive:** You seek continuous improvement opportunities, learn from your mistakes and refuse to get into self-pity or blame others for your mistakes.

- **You respect individual differences:** You acknowledge the fact that people are all different and have varying needs. Respect others' points of views that are different from yours and accommodate situations that are not favorable to your personal beliefs.

- **You feel very comfortable in social conditions:** You are comfortable dealing with a crowd or occupying a spot under the limelight. You enjoy deserved praise and know how to show off in front of people without bragging much about what you have or what you can do.

- **You see challenges as opportunities for improvement:** Rather than fall into self-pity or despair when faced with a challenge, you think creatively of innovative approaches to solve or use the challenge to create a positive impact in your life and that of others.

- **You are not discouraged by defeat or failure:** You seek the root cause of each defeat or failure and learn lessons for performance improvement. As such each defeat or failure is an opportunity to learn and do better.

- **When frustrated you demonstrate emotional stability with the ability to cope:** When you are hurt or feel let down by someone else or yourself, you don't react immediately. You intentionally stay silent for time enough to reflect, meditate and build necessary positive energy to change your mindset from negative to positive. This restores your self-efficacy required to overcome the frustration.

- **You demonstrate motivation and commitment when it comes to obligations:** You see every obligation as an opportunity to thrive and trust yourself to be up to the task. You seek solutions from within striving to be innovative and seek help from the right persons while demonstrating   creativity   and

independence.

Once you identify your confidence gaps the next
step is to seek for assistance to close the gaps or
boost your self-confidence.

We shall provide some tips but sometimes you
may need coaching and mentoring to close the
gaps and attain your fullest potential. It is also
possible to use the tips for self-coaching with the
support of a mentor or a role model.

Positive energy is all that you need

CLOSING YOUR GAP
(Tips for building and boosting self-confidence)

Aim high & shoot highest: let your achievements surpass your dreams

After conducting your confidence level assessment, you must have identified some gaps. You can use some of the following tips through self-coaching to close the gaps where applicable:

- Take a leap out of your comfort zone. You could try acquiring a new skill, a new hobby, getting to meet persons you haven't met before and expand your network. These should be actions that lead you towards your goals.

- Set realistic and attainable goals and think positive.

- Practice a good posture at all times especially when you are walking alone. There is what is termed a "confidence posture": walking straight and smart, stand straight with your stomach tugged in. Look confident and sure of yourself.

- Stay well groomed: neat, well and decently dressed, nice simple make-up and hair kept neat and nice and keep fresh fragrance always.

- Create your unique style in dressing, create your own standard that you are comfortable and confident with. Don't attempt to follow the crowd.

- Don't care about what people think about you as long as you are convinced you are doing the right thing and it's not hurting anybody. Never be scared to do what is right.

- Personalize your look, be unique and confident: jewelry, hairstyle, shoes, purse and any other accessories.

- Keep your room clean, organized and cozy.

- Always have pads/tampons in your bag at all times, change pads regularly to prevent staining your dress.

- Be up to date with your class work and ask questions to ensure you are following up. Don't be shy to ask clarification questions. It's your right!

- Avoid using slangs especially in class.

- Develop talents such as dancing, sports, fashion and design, culinary skills, theatre.

- Join school clubs that can help you develop your social skills, if necessary.

- Participate in your hobbies such as music, reading, poetry, painting, drawing and swimming.

- Let go of friends who do not respect you nor like you as you are. If someone makes you feel bad or not good enough then they are not your friends and you should end the friendship.

- Make friends with people you like and not those that you think you should be friends with.

- Understand that it is not healthy that your peers should walk all over you. Say NO when necessary.

- Embrace differences in others; stay nice and courteous towards people.

- Socialize and make friends with your parents, converse with adults while being polite. You will learn wisdom.

- Understand that it is very bad to be pressured into having a relationship or dating when you are not ready.

- Never be pressured into doing drugs, getting drunk, or having sex. While in a state of drunkenness or drugged up, you lose self-control and can-do things that you will regret.

- Be yourself. Be beautiful for yourself and not so as to be like someone else.

- Get over any slights and don't take insults to mind.

- Take compliments graciously.

- Encourage yourself. Look at yourself in the mirror and compliment your looks and don't compare yourself with someone else.

- If in a bad mood, ask for help from a trusted source. Your emotional health is very necessary for making good decisions.

- Avoid confrontations.

Watch out!!!

- Say no if something doesn't feel right or seems dangerous. Stay away from self-destructive people who get into drugs, vandalism or gangs.

- You have the right to end any hateful conversations. Just walk away.

- Do not overdo it if you are not liked by some people. Keep a sense of humor about yourself.

- Being confident means not caving into peer pressure. You make up your own mind about things.

- Avoid acting arrogantly to hide your insecurities. Most people don't like it and can see through it.

- If you're having serious problems with a close friend, don't start a fight. Calm down and use your words. Talk it out and respect their feelings. Treat them with dignity. Tell them you expect them to be always honest with you.

Sometimes self-coaching may not be sufficient to close your confidence gaps. Don't be shy, ask for help from trusted sources which include your parents or a role-model who can play the role of your mentor.

Bibiana Mbuh Taku

Challenges should feed creativity & innovation

PARENTS: COACH, MENTOR, ROLE MODEL

Parents, be a catalyst and not the driver

There are several approaches to the teenage girl's confidence building and a good blend of the three approaches could be quite effective:

- Parenting
- Coaching
- Mentoring

Role-modeling could be imbedded into the three approaches. From my experience, tweens and teens learn better from someone they look-up to and admire. They are more willing to be coached and mentored by a person they know, trust and admire than by a total stranger be it an expert or not.

Let's examine the role of each approach though they nearly always work together in a mix that is specific to each case:

❖ **PARENTING**

This is the most effective and impactful approach to confidence building since a parent can be the coach, the mentor and the role model. Children will easily imitate their parents and trust their parents to love them unconditionally. Coaching and mentoring could be built into parenting and effected through formal and informal discussions and role-modelling.

I recently had a discussion with two separate groups of young people:

• The first group was a group of 8 female graduates within the bracket of 24 to 30 years, holders of master degrees, participants in a focus group discussion on "Strong confident women and leadership".

I asked each of them to name at least one strong confident and successful woman whom they know, who is their role model and influencer.

The first example for each of the eight girls was their mother. The personality trait that made them their role model ranged from: self-sufficiency, independence, hardworking, focused and determined, kind and empathetic, goal-oriented, honesty, belief in themselves and resilience. Some of the girls added that their fathers were very supportive and have contributed enormously to build their self-confidence.

Their fathers can carry out every type of discussion with them, coach and uplift them when they feel like they have let him down. Their fathers have been their chief cheerleaders.

They inspire them to look forward to being respected by their boyfriend or husband if and when they get married, by treating their mothers with love, respect and support towards achieving their goals.

• The second group of young people were 20 young persons between the ages of 8 to 13 at a holiday camp made up of 5 boys and 13 girls. Our topic of discussion was on the empowerment of the girl-child and getting boys to be supportive.

I asked them to give an example of at least one woman who inspires them most and why and their response for both boys and girls was their mothers first, and then for some the proprietor of the holiday camp, and then some others their aunts.

The reason why these persons inspire them included: Intelligence, wisdom, beauty, cleanliness and orderliness, kindness, self-confidence, generosity, dressing and overall physical presentation and ability to protect them.

The result of these discussions with the two groups of young people highlights the effectiveness of parents' role-modelling. Embedding self-confidence building tips, coaching and mentoring into parenting could go a long way to boost the confidence level of a teenage girl and proactively reduce the gap.

The following tips can be helpful:

- Teach your tween and teenage girl how to balance self-acceptance with self-improvement.
- Praise her efforts instead of the outcome.
- Teach her assertiveness skills.
- Encourage her to explore new opportunities.
- Role-model self-confidence to her.
  Build self-worth on a healthy foundation, she needs to love herself and personalize her values rather than succumbing to peer pressure and seeking approval or acceptance
- Balance freedom with guidance.

- Guide her to develop positive self-talk or affirmations.

❖ *COACHING*

Coaching can be built into parenting. The teenage girl can be empowered for self-coaching through parenting or school programs.

However, in special circumstances, there may be a need for an external coach or counsel.

These are situations in which parenting has been insufficient to help the teenage girl close her confidence gaps.

The parents may be overwhelmed, were not prepared for the changes resulting from adolescence, are unavailable or the relationship has broken down for one reason or another.

In such cases, specialist coaching or counseling may be sought.

Specialized programs or services can diagnose the root cause of the confidence gap or loss of self-esteem and self-efficacy.

Once the indicators and the root causes are identified a program will be put in place to coach and counsel the girl to regain and boost her self-confidence.

The following are a sample of themes that can be found in counseling programs of the teen girl, and the choice of the theme will be based on the identified need to be addressed:

- Learn to love yourself despite your circumstances
- Learn to accept your human imperfections
- Increase your self-confidence
- Become empowered to make changes

- Reaffirm your self-worth & improve your self-esteem
- Increased self-esteem and self- awareness
- Improved decision-making ability
- Enhanced relationship with parents
- Better communication skills
- New friendships
- Improved grades and work ethic
- Organization and time management skills
- An understanding of choices and consequences
- Future planning and vision
- Realization of potential and goals
- Positive self-expression and self-acceptance

The challenge of using counseling services or programs include the unwillingness of the teenage girl to open up and collaborate with a stranger on very personal and intimate issues. Counseling can succeed if the counselor is able to break the barrier, and strikes some amount of friendship and build trust with the girl. On the other hand, if the relationship with the parents is broken, there will be a need to repair the relationship, counsel the parent(s), support the parents to use appropriate parenting coaching, mentoring and role-modeling to help the girl.

❖ MENTORING

Mentoring is indispensable for a healthy and successful transition of the girl-child from tween age through teenage to adulthood. She doesn't have to be in crisis before needing mentoring. Her first mentors are the parents and then other members of the close family or the household, in our cultural context.

This number expands usually to include the class teacher, especially the female class teacher.

However, the primary responsibility to provide mentoring to the girl lies on her parents who need to consciously understand her and accompany her through stages of her development.

They are the first persons that she trusts, and trust is the rock on which mentoring sits.

The girl-child tries to imitate her mother and if nothing happens to dampen that admiration then she will continue to be her role model and de facto mentor. The bond between her and her father is naturally so strong that she sees her father as one who loves her unconditionally, and she loves him back the same. His opinion counts so much that advice from her father is accepted without a second thought.

The goal is to maintain her trust by always upholding his word and being honest as much as possible. He is, therefore, her greatest source of inspiration and mentor.

However, mentoring and role modeling through parenting may sometimes become insufficient as she interacts more and more with a variety of persons who exert some influence on her and her values such as peers at school.

This can be compounded by parents becoming too busy to pay attention and provide appropriate coaching and mentoring to boost her declining self-confidence through coping skills. At this moment concerted mentoring plan with complete buy-in from the girl herself needs to be put in place.

This plan may be steered by the girl herself with guidance from her parents or external mentor if necessary. Whatever the case may be, it is necessary to provide mentoring to every teenage girl and such mentoring starts during tween age to prepare her for puberty and enforced during puberty to boost her declining self-confidence and raise it to its optimum.

The following tips are helpful for mentoring of teenage girls:

- Agree to a convenient schedule.
- Build and sustain mutual trust.
- Listen and be non-judgmental.
- Be consistently empathetic.
- Encourage and celebrate every achievement and improvement.
- Demonstrate that you have faith in them and encourage them to come out of their comfort zone.

Mentoring could be mixed with coaching and role-modelling for counselling girls whose low self-confidence leads to a crisis requiring the intervention of expert and experienced counselling services.

The above approaches, as we said earlier on can potentially be developed into a blended approach or mix to produce an efficient and effective confidence building or boosting strategy. There can't be a standard mix, but each mix is specific to a case and context.

A girl who has successfully closed her confidence gap, and developed resilience to be able to transform her greatest challenges into opportunities to boost her self-esteem to the optimum, is best armed to empower others. She is a potential peer mentor.

Be that confident girl

Let your light shine; hold other hands!

Bibiana Mbuh Taku

ARE YOU A CONFIDENT GIRL?

EMPOWER OTHERS.
BECOME A PEER MENTOR

Be an influencer and not an influenced. Take the first step.

"Develop enough courage so that you can stand up for yourself and then stand up for somebody else"
(Dr. Maya Angelou)

I was raised by a single mother from a broken polygamous home. My mother, Helen ATABONG ASABA was born into one of the strongest and most revered royal families of my village. She was the most senior daughter of her father Prince ASABA NYIAWUNG FONTEM the eldest son of His Royal Majesty, the feared and revered Fontem ASONGANYI.

She was unconditionally loved and cherished by her father and her grandfather. She was groomed by both men to enjoy the privileges of male princes as well as their responsibilities. This privileged status came with enormous challenges compounded with her marriage to my polygamous father, MBETAKU, who was a noble man and a firearms producer for the wars that the monarch fought and won.

The numerous delicate diplomatic missions that she undertook on behalf of her famous grandfather and her father gave her opportunities to develop high self-efficacy and self-esteem skills. She became the first woman to be the successor of a man, her father — a prince, with rights to landed property.

My mother became the defender and crusader of the economic human rights of women while championing the right to education for all children irrespective of gender.

My mother was a de facto coach, mentor and role-model to many whose self-confidence was crushed in one way or another. One of the sayings, which she used when a child was going through a confidence crisis, was: *"there is no bad tadpole in the river"*.

In other words, no child is so bad as to not deserve being given many chances. She succeeded in coaching and mentoring many parents to turn their kids around. She was their role-model having succeeded in turning her own kids around.

This is a true story of a non-literate girl-child turned strong, successful and empathetic female leader who acquired coaching skills and, mentoring skills and, built resilience and in turn used them to empower several persons and, left a legacy of an incredible influencer. She is not a singular case there are many others. You could be the next.

Do you know that you could champion peer mentoring? You are a confident girl and have experiences that you could use to encourage and empower your peers whose self-confidence is declining.

Your story could be a resource and serve as an authentic source of hope that it is possible to re-build lost self-esteem, self-worth and self-efficacy.

Peer mentors are efficient because they can easily relate with their peers whose stories are familiar. You can easily build the trust required for effective mentoring.

However, you need support from an experienced mentor who can groom you through coaching, mentoring and experience sharing. You could also take a course in mentoring as a hobby or a career.

The generations of successful confident women that the world dearly needs are women that are strong and resilient enough to hold many hands not only of women but also of men. They can effectively lead themselves, are creative and innovative and, are able to role-model, influence and lead others. They trust their capabilities and abilities and are resilient enough to weather any storms and thrive through adversity.

Bibiana Mbuh Taku

Are you ready?

BE THAT CONFIDENT GIRL!

Be that confident girl

My mother my model and coach

ACKNOWLEDGMENTS

I want to sincerely thank all those who have contributed in putting this handbook together:

- Marie Angele ABANGA, my daughter and a serial author patiently put her graphic design skills to work.
- Pauline N. FOY and Beatrice ACHALEKE, another serial author, my daughters edited the scripts.
- Mr. Samuel T. WELANG, a seasoned educationist did not only write a very befitting foreword. He is an unsung hero in counselling and transformation of young people.
- Mrs. Pauline N. WELANG wrote an introduction that highlighted her perfect knowledge of the experience we share in the empowerment of the woman and the girl child.
- Mr. BIDIAS, one of the best illustrators I have worked with.
- Therese ATABONG my daughter provided me some invaluable content.

- My brother and friend, Chief Barrister Charles ACHALEKE TAKU, provided me the invaluable moral support.

I am very grateful for my entire household led by Lady Ursula FONTEM & Melissa TAKU for the incredible support and encouragement.

ABOUT THE AUTHOR

Bibiana Mbuh Taku is a confident English-speaking Cameroonian. I have known Bibiana since 1977 when we met in the then Business School of the University Centre of Douala struggling to take lessons in French, understand in English, write and pass tests and examinations. Thus, competing with the majority of French-speaking colleagues on their own terms.

She was married with a baby and had a second baby while going to school and running her house. We were attracted to each other by our common challenges as women and Anglophones learning in a difficult environment. Her determination to stay focused and strive to succeed against all odds is something I saw in her and admired, and which is her trademark.

Resilience is a life skill that both of us developed from our under-privileged backgrounds which we used to not only survive but thrive in a context where the learning language was un-favorable but failure was not an option. Bibiana possesses strong academic credentials and a career profile that is intricate.

Bibiana graduated from the Business school top in her batch. She worked for American life insurance company briefly, and then joined Pecten Cameroon Company where we both worked as financial analysts. She has been an advocate of continuous improvement through seeking out challenges including learning new skills and leaving her comfort zone to meander through several sectors in varying roles.

She later went to The National School of Administration and Magistracy (ENAM) where she also graduated top in her batch. She has worked as a Treasury Inspector and chief of service for accounts and cash, then worked for Plan

International as the Operations Support Manager.

In 2009, she finally set out to do what she loved most, founding a limited liability Consultancy, Diversity Management & Consulting as the chief executive officer and consultant. She is a senior Business Development Consultant, Certified Master Trainer for IFC-LPI, certified TPMA assessor and a certified Instructional designer. She is also a Scope insight Trainer of Agricultural Organisations Assessors.

She is a passionate advocate and champion of the economic empowerment of youths, girls and women. She inherited this passion from her mother that I also came to know very well in our friendship, who role-modeled self-confidence and resilience to Bibiana and fought confidently to send her to school, and to protect her rights as a woman in a patriarchal society.

Bibiana has braved it through life's ups and downs with confidence and ability to transform challenges and adversity into opportunities to stand for herself and for others.

Today, she is not only an entrepreneur par excellence, but she is also a humanitarian activist. She is the founder and program director of the Helen Atabong Asaba Foundation (founded after her beloved mother).

She is also the founder of the Gabriel Bebonbechem Foundation for Epilepsy and Mental Well-being to fight against stigmatization of persons living with Epilepsy and mental illness. This foundation is in memory of her son who died after living with epilepsy and mental illness.

She recently launched a program for the empowerment of the woman and the girl child called "Coach and Mentor a Girl to Thrive" (CAMGTT). The maiden edition of the one-month pilot program was earlier this year when 10 girls were coached and mentored based on the gaps identified throughout the program.

The author is a mother of 3 biological daughters and many natural daughters, grandmother of 7 biological grandchildren and many natural grandchildren. She coaches and mentors many children, youths and, women and is very passionate about all she does including working in her garden.

I am happy to introduce Bibiana who has come a long way in role-modelling creativity, building self-confidence, resilience, and sharing her experiences, with the society at large. She has diligently put some of her core values into this book **"BE THAT CONFIDENT GIRL"**.

Pauline WELANG
Retired Finance Director/Cameroon Development Corporation (CDC)

Be that confident girl

CEO Buea Shopping Mall & LINA's

PERSONAL NOTES OF THE CONFIDENT GIRL HERE!

Printed in Great Britain
by Amazon